Lady Gaga

By Molly Aloian

Crabtree Publishing Company

www.crabtreebooks.com

Crabtree Publishing Company
www.crabtreebooks.com

Author: Molly Aloian
Publishing plan research and development:
  Sean Charlebois, Reagan Miller
  Crabtree Publishing Company
Project coordinator: Kathy Middleton
Photo research: Crystal Sikkens
Editor: Crystal Sikkens
Designer: Ken Wright
Production coordinator and Prepress
  technician: Ken Wright

Photographs:
Associated Press: page 23
Dreamstime: page 1
Getty Images: Daniel Boczarski/Contributor/
  Referns: page 16; Kevin Mazur/Contributor/
  WireImage: page 26
Keystone Press: PBG/EMPICS Entertainment:
  cover; Zumapress.com: pages 6, 7, 9, 24;
  ABACA USA/EMPICS Entertainment:
  pages 8, 20; Nancy Kaszerman/KPA-ZUMA:
  page 10; wenn.com: pages 12, 15, 25; Doug
  Peters/EMPICS Entertainment: page 13;
  Mavrixphoto.com: page 19; BIG Pictures UK:
  page 27
Shutterstock: pages 4, 5, 17, 21, 28
Wikimedia Commons: atp_tyreseus: page 11

Every effort has been made to trace copyright holders and to obtain their permission for use of copyright material. The authors and publishers would be pleased to rectify any error or omission in future editions. All the Internet addresses given in this book were correct at the time of going to press. The author and publishers regret any inconvenience caused if addresses have changed or sites have ceased to exist, but can accept no responsibility for any such changes.

Library and Archives Canada Cataloguing in Publication

Aloian, Molly
  Lady Gaga / Molly Aloian.

(Superstars!)
Includes index.
Issued also in electronic formats.
ISBN 978-0-7787-7609-3 (bound).--ISBN 978-0-7787-7614-7 (pbk.)

  1. Lady Gaga--Juvenile literature. 2. Singers--United States--
Biography--Juvenile literature. I. Title. II. Series: Superstars!
(St. Catharines, Ont.)

ML3930.L157L15 2011   j782.42164092   C2011-905594-5

Library of Congress Cataloging-in-Publication Data

Aloian, Molly.
  Lady Gaga / by Molly Aloian.
    p. cm. -- (Superstars!)
  Includes index.
  ISBN 978-0-7787-7609-3 (reinforced library binding : alk. paper) --
ISBN 978-0-7787-7614-7 (pbk. : alk. paper) -- ISBN 978-1-4271-8855-7
(electronic pdf) -- ISBN 978-1-4271-9758-0 (electronic html)
  1. Lady Gaga--Juvenile literature. 2. Singers--United States--
Biography--Juvenile literature. I. Title. II. Series.

ML3930.L13A56 2012
782.42164092--dc23
[B]
                                                        2011032464

Crabtree Publishing Company

www.crabtreebooks.com   1-800-387-7650

Printed in Canada/082011/MA20110714

Published in Canada
Crabtree Publishing
616 Welland Ave.
St. Catharines, ON
L2M 5V6

Published in the United States
Crabtree Publishing
PMB 59051
350 Fifth Avenue, 59th Floor
New York, New York 10118

Published in the United Kingdom
Crabtree Publishing
Maritime House
Basin Road North, Hove
BN41 1WR

Published in Australia
Crabtree Publishing
3 Charles Street
Coburg North
VIC 3058

CONTENTS

Words that are defined in the glossary are in
bold type the first time they appear in the text.

Everyone's Gone Gaga

There's no denying it: Lady Gaga is a household name. A talented singer, songwriter, fashion **icon**, and **activist**, she has captivated audiences around the world and has millions of adoring and devoted fans. Her very first album, called *The Fame*, sold more than 14 million copies worldwide. She has toured the globe, playing sold-out shows in the United States, Europe, and Asia—everywhere from Miami, Florida, to Tokyo, Japan, to London, United Kingdom. She has been called one of the most exciting artists of the 21st century! She has met Queen Elizabeth and been interviewed by Oprah!

Nice to Meat You

Lady Gaga is known for her flamboyant costumes on stage and off. One of her most memorable outfits to date is a 35-pound (15.8 kg) dress made entirely out of raw meat (left). She wore the dress to the 2010 MTV Video Music Awards. Her famous outfit was on display at the Rock and Roll Hall of Fame in July of 2011.

Rocky Road

Gaga got her big break in early 2009, but success did not come easy to the pop singer. In high school, Gaga was teased mercilessly for being different and for her interest in art and music. Today, she is still fighting a battle against critics, listeners, and other musicians who claim that she is merely an attention-seeker and not a true artist.

She Said It

"[I was] teased for being ugly, having a big nose, being annoying. 'Your laugh is funny, you're weird, why do you always sing, why are you so into theater, why do you do your make-up like that?'... I didn't even want to go to school sometimes."
—In an interview in *Rolling Stone* magazine, 2011

Queen of Pop

Lady Gaga was born Stefani Joanne Angelina Germanotta. It was the popular 1984 song "Radio Ga Ga" that **inspired** her stage name. A British rock group called Queen wrote the song. The band's front man and main songwriter, Freddie Mercury, was also known for his flamboyant spirit. He died of **AIDS** in 1991 and Queen was inducted into the Rock and Roll Hall of Fame in 2001.

This picture shows Lady Gaga holding a Queen album.

She Said It

"I adored Freddie Mercury and Queen had a hit called Radio Gaga. That's why I love the name... Freddie was unique—one of the biggest personalities in the whole of pop music."
—In an interview with www.dailyrecord.co.uk, November 2009

Gaga Speaks Out

Gaga's music, videos, and over-the-top, outrageous performances have earned her numerous awards and landed her on the covers of many popular fashion and entertainment magazines. The Grammy winner is also an outspoken **advocate** for **social justice** and **equality**. In June of 2011, at a gay rights event in Rome, Italy, she demanded the end of **intolerance** and **discrimination** against gay people. She told the crowd of an estimated one million people, "Let us be **revolutionaries** of love and use our very strong human powers to save lives and encourage unity around the world." Her song "Born This Way" has been called a gay anthem. An anthem is a special song that unites a group of people and expresses their identity.

BORN TO BE

Lady Gaga's single "Born This Way," from her second full-length album of the same name, reached the number one spot in 19 countries around the world, and was the fastest-selling single in the history of iTunes. It sold one million copies in just five days.

Lady Gaga speaks out during the Gay Pride concert in Rome on June 11, 2011.

Growing Up Gaga

Stefani Joanne Angelina Germanotta was born in Yonkers, New York on March 28, 1986, to Italian-American parents Joseph and Cynthia Germanotta. Her younger sister Natali was born on March 10, 1992. Joseph and Cynthia were supportive parents and encouraged both of their daughters to pursue their dreams. In the first grade Stefani won the role of big billy goat in the play *Three Billy Goats Gruff*. She made her own goat horns out of tin foil and clothes hangers and stole the show. Natali noticed her older sister's determination and ambition even when they were kids. Natali would sometimes ask, "Why do you always have to be the best?"

Lady Gaga and her sister attended the 2011 CFDA Awards.

Side-by-Side Sisters

On June 6, 2011, Lady Gaga and her younger sister attended the 2011 Council of Fashion Designers of America (CFDA) Fashion Awards at Alice Tully Hall, Lincoln Center in New York City. Gaga was honored with the award for Fashion Icon of the Year. She thanked Natali in her acceptance speech.

Musical Ear

When she was four years old, Stefani began learning how to play the piano. She hated her lessons and practicing scales, but she loved playing by ear. Her lessons paid off in the end, however, as she became very good at classical piano. By age 13, she had written her first piano ballad. A ballad is a type of song. She also loved pop music and enjoyed singing along with Michael Jackson, Cyndi Lauper, and Madonna.

This Lady Gaga fan is celebrating the first official Lady Gaga Day in Taichung, Taiwan, on July 3, 2011.

LITTLE MONSTERS

Lady Gaga calls her fans her "little monsters." She has some of the most devoted fans on the planet. Her fans idolize her, **emulate** her, and want to purchase all things Gaga-related. She has over 5 million followers on Twitter and over 10 million friends on Facebook.

Catholic School Days

Joseph and Cynthia enrolled Stefani in a private all-girls Catholic school called the Convent of the Sacred Heart. Located on the Upper East Side of Manhattan, the school was very **exclusive** and tuition was extremely expensive. Other students during that time included Niki and Paris Hilton. Stefani's parents wanted their daughter to have the best education money could buy. She participated in high school musicals, portraying the lead roles of Adelaide in *Guys and Dolls* and Philia in *A Funny Thing Happened on the Way to the Forum*. She also played the role of Alice More in *A Man For All Seasons*.

Lady Gaga's vocal coach, Don Lawrence, is shown here at the BMI Urban Awards.

Thanks, Coach!

Stefani also started working with a famous voice coach named Don Lawrence. Beyoncé, Christina Aguilera, and En Vogue were some of his other students. Don was aware of Stefani's special musical talents and helped her grow as both a singer and an artist. He was a source of support and inspiration throughout Stefani's entire journey from awkward schoolgirl to pop queen.

Pass the Mic

As a teenager, Stefani wrote all kinds of songs and performed at open mic nights at clubs in Manhattan. An open mic is a live show during which audience members may perform at the microphone. Her appetite for music, art, and fashion was getting bigger and bigger. She listened to David Bowie and Queen, and admired Grace Jones's unique style and great music.

This picture shows the Tisch School of the Arts in New York City.

Taking On Tisch

At the age of 17, Stefani was accepted into the **prestigious** Tisch School of the Arts at New York University. Tisch is one of 15 schools that make up New York University. There, she studied music and worked on her songwriting skills by composing essay papers that focused on topics such as art, religion, and politics. Angelina Jolie, Anne Hathaway, and Selma Blair are among the other celebrities that attended Tisch.

Welcome to the Neighborhood

In the second semester of her sophomore year, Stefani withdrew from Tisch so she could focus all her attention on her musical career. Her father agreed to pay her rent for one full year, on the condition that she would return to her studies at Tisch if she did not have success with her singing and songwriting. She moved to New York's East Village. This trendy, artistic neighborhood attracted all kind of musicians. Many of Stefani's musical and artistic idols, such as Madonna and Andy Warhol, spent time in the East Village at some point in their careers.

Lady Gaga performed at The Slipper Room in New York in 2007.

She Said It

"I wasn't signed to a label, it was just stuff I was doing in New York. That's the kind of girl I am. I never waited for somebody to hand me something on a silver platter. I was like, 'I wanna make a record, OK, so I'll save up my money and buy a four-track tape recorder.' I used to just hustle, I'd grind, I'd do whatever I had to do."
—From *Just Dance: The Biography*, 2010

Beginning at the Bitter End

In 2005, Stefani formed a band called SGBand. They played their first live performance at a nightclub in Greenwich Village called The Bitter End. Shortly after, Stefani recorded a five-track demo called *Words*. She then decided to record and release her first EP. It was called *Red & Blue* and featured songs called "Something Crazy," "Wish You Were Here," "No Floods," "Words," and "Red & Blue." She launched the EP at The Bitter End in 2006.

VIVA GAGA

In 2010, Lady Gaga joined forces with Cyndi Lauper and MAC Cosmetics. They launched a line of lipstick under MAC's supplementary cosmetic line called Viva Glam. All the net proceeds of the lipstick line, called Viva Glam Gaga and Viva Glam Cyndi respectively, were donated to the cosmetic company's campaign to prevent HIV and AIDS worldwide.

Lady Gaga attended the MAC Viva Glam launch in March of 2010.

A Meeting of the Minds

The EP was a huge success and Stefani was chosen to be one of nine performers at the 2006 New Songwriters Showcase at The Cutting Room in New York. At the showcase, she met a famous producer from Sony named Rob Fusari. Fusari helped launch the group Destiny's Child and had worked with a wide range of artists including Will Smith and pop icons Britney Spears and Jessica Simpson. Stefani and Rob worked well together and he found her sense of theater and drama fascinating. The pair wrote songs together and Stefani kept performing live, allowing her show to change and grow.

NAME GAME

One afternoon while they were working in the studio, Fusari compared Stefani to Freddie Mercury because of her flair for the dramatic. He called her "Gaga," which was a reference to the Queen song called "Radio Ga Ga." Stefani loved the name and even her mother started calling her Gaga. It was official: she was now Lady Gaga.

She Said It

"Lady Gaga is my name. If you know me, and you call me Stefani, you don't really know me at all."
—In an interview for *New York* magazine (2010)

Two Ladies

Lady Starlight, another performance artist in New York, influenced Lady Gaga and helped her develop her on-stage **persona**. She encouraged Gaga to push her creativity and live performances to the limit. The two also performed a show together called Lady Gaga and The Starlight Revue or simply "the ultimate pop burlesque rock show" throughout the spring and summer of 2007. It included singing, go-go dancing, and other forms of performance art. Their first gig was at Gaga's favorite club The Bitter End.

Lady Gaga and Lady Starlight performed together in 2007.

The Ladies at Lollapalooza

In August of 2007, Lady Gaga and Lady Starlight were booked to perform at one of the largest music festivals in the United States—Lollapalooza. Gaga sang nine songs she had written, including the unreleased song called "Blueberry Kisses," as well as songs that would eventually be part of her **debut** album *The Fame*, including "Boys, Boys, Boys" and "Beautiful, Dirty, Rich."

This picture shows Lady Gaga performing at Lollapalooza in 2007.

She Said It

"All the stuff you see Lady Gaga do now—the fire and fog and the elaborate outfits—were things we wanted to do, but we didn't have any money. We tried to give our outfits as much visual impact as possible for the least amount of cash. That usually involved going to the fabric store and buying mirrors, sequins, fringe and then gluing it on to our underwear…[Lady Gaga] wanted to do something different and exciting visually. That's where I came into the picture…It was really more of my attitude towards art that was influential to her, rather than any specific look or style. Do it as big as you can, as loud as you can. Whatever it is. The more shocking the better."
—Lady Starlight, www.popeater.com

Writing Songs

In 2007, Interscope signed Lady Gaga as a songwriter. She was hired to write songs for Britney Spears, New Kids on the Block, Fergie, the Pussycat Dolls, and other performers. While Gaga was writing at Interscope, a recording artist and songwriter called Akon recognized her talents as a singer. He had his own record label called Konvict Muzik.

Rapper Akon was born in Senegal in western Africa.

RedOne

Akon was also involved in another side project with a record producer and songwriter called RedOne, with whom Lady Gaga also worked alongside. In fact, she produced the song "Boys, Boys, Boys" with RedOne. Konvict was set up with RedOne to write music for established artists. Lady Gaga worked in the studio with Akon on songs for the forthcoming Pussycat Dolls album called *Doll Domination*. She also continued to collaborate with RedOne.

The Fame Begins

By 2008, Lady Gaga was living in Los Angeles, where she was working on her debut album *The Fame.* Interscope released the first single "Just Dance" in April of 2008. In total, she had spent two and a half years working on *The Fame* with RedOne and other producers and songwriters.

Slow Climb

In the United States, "Just Dance" spent almost five months on the Billboard Hot 100 before finally reaching the top of the chart in January of 2009. It scored the third-biggest single-week total of all time, selling over 400,000 downloads in just one week. It went on to become the second best-selling digital song of all time in the United States. Today, "Just Dance" is among the best-selling singles of all time, selling over 7.7 million copies. The album reached number one in countries such as the United Kingdom, Canada, Austria, Germany, Switzerland, and Ireland. In the United States, the album peaked at number two on the Billboard 200 and topped Billboard's Dance/Electronic Albums chart.

She Said It

"This idea of 'the fame' runs through and through…Basically, if you have nothing—no money, no fame—you can still feel beautiful and dirty rich. It's about making choices, and having references—things you pull from your life that you believe in. It's about self-discovery and being creative."
—From www.mtv.com, 2008

On Tour

Interscope sent Lady Gaga on tour with the New Kids on the Block sold-out reunion tour. It was one of the biggest tours in the fall of 2008. This was Gaga's first time performing in large arenas and other venues that held thousands of people. The tour began in Los Angeles on October 8 and continued until the end of November.

Lady Gaga opens for NKOTB in Fort Lauderdale, Florida, in 2008.

First Album

The Fame was released on October 28, 2008. Other singles on the album included "Eh, Eh (Nothing Else I Can Say)," "LoveGame," "Poker Face," and "Paparazzi." Lady Gaga promoted the album by performing the songs in several live appearances, including her first headlining worldwide concert tour called The Fame Ball Tour. Gaga described the tour as "the first-ever pop electro opera."

RISING STAR

In October, Gaga received *Billboard* magazine's Rising Star of 2009 award. During the same month, she attended the Human Rights Campaign's national dinner and then marched in the National Equality March for the equal protection of lesbian, gay, bisexual, and **transgendered** people in Washington, D.C.

> Lady Gaga promotes her album *The Fame* at a press conference at the Grand Intercontinental Hotel in Seoul, South Korea.

Becoming Famous

The Fame has won numerous awards since it was released in 2008. In total, the album and its songs have been nominated for six Grammy Awards, including Album of the Year. It went on to win the Grammy Award for Best Electronic/Dance Album and "Poker Face" won Best Dance Recording. *The Fame* also won Best International Album at the 2010 BRIT Awards.

Lady Gaga performs during her Monster Ball Tour.

The Fame Monster

On November 18, 2009, Gaga released *The Fame Monster*. Four days after the release, her second tour called The Monster Ball Tour commenced. *The Fame Monster* contained just eight songs that dealt with the darker side of fame. On December 15, 2009, a Super Deluxe version of *The Fame Monster* containing the two albums, as well as additional **merchandise** including a lock from one of her wigs, was released. *The Fame Monster* won the Grammy for Best Pop Vocal Album and The Monster Ball Tour was a huge commercial and critical success. According to *Billboard* magazine, the tour **grossed** over 200 million dollars, making it one of the highest-grossing concert tours of all time.

Pop Queen

By the time she released *Born This Way* in 2011, Lady Gaga was a staple in the pop music world and beyond. She had been named one of *Time* magazine's 100 Most Influential People of the Year, performed on numerous talk shows, appeared in hundreds of fashion and entertainment magazines, received countless nominations and awards for her songs and videos, was a full-blown fashion **innovator** and icon, as well as a celebrated human rights activist.

Haus of Gaga

Gaga works very hard on every detail in her music videos and live shows. She also strives to maintain her unique persona both on stage and off. In 2008, Lady Gaga began working with a creative team called the Haus of Gaga. The Haus works behind-the-scenes and is made up of artists, designers, and creative people who travel with Gaga on tour and help her make her musical and artistic ideas come to life. They design the sets and stage props for her live shows and music videos, design her costumes and hairstyles, and act as sounding boards for her ideas. Many critics believe that the Haus is modeled on Andy Warhol's New York art studio, which was called The Factory.

He Said It

*"We hear Lady Gaga's music everywhere we go. It is like a soundtrack of our times…In addition to her **formidable** songwriting skills, she is a modern fashion **phenomenon**."*
—Giorgio Armani, 2011

Album Announcement

Gaga announced the name of her much-anticipated new album *Born This Way* during her acceptance speech for Video of the Year at the 2010 MTV Video Music Awards, while wearing her infamous meat dress. Her video for "Bad Romance" took the award. The song "Telephone" featuring Beyoncé Knowles, was also nominated for the award.

A Meaty Statement

Artist and fashion designer Franc Fernandez and Gaga's stylist Nicola Formichetti worked together to create Lady Gaga's meat dress. The dress took two days to complete and Gaga had to be stitched into it backstage. She wore the dress once more on the *Ellen DeGeneres Show*. *Time* magazine voted the meat dress as the top fashion statement of 2010, but animal rights activists were alarmed and upset by Gaga's fashion choice.

Lady Gaga accepts the award for Video of the Year at the MTV Video Music Awards on Sept. 12, 2010.

23

Gaga's Grammys

The single "Born This Way" was released in February of 2011 before the release of the album. It was Gaga's third single to top the Billboard Hot 100 chart and spent a total of six weeks on the chart. Lady Gaga first performed the song at the 53rd Grammy Awards, where she won the award for Best Pop Vocal Performance for "Bad Romance," as well as two other Grammys. Gaga sang "Born This Way" after emerging from an egg-shaped vessel that was carried onto the red carpet.

Lady Gaga arrived at the 53rd annual Grammy Awards in the vessel, which was carried by models and dancers.

The Vessel

A fashion designer named Hussein Chalayan designed Lady Gaga's somewhat see-through vessel. Chalayan was born in Nicosia, which is the capital city of Cyprus, but moved to England with his family in 1978. He is **renowned** for his innovative use of materials. He was also the inspiration behind "the living dress," which was a shape-shifting outfit Gaga wore during The Monster Ball Tour.

Single Success

The singles "Judas" and "The Edge of Glory" were released shortly after "Born This Way." "Judas" was criticized for its religious references to Judas, Mary Magdalene, and Jesus Christ, but the song still debuted at number 30 on the Billboard Pop Songs chart and eventually landed in the top ten on the Billboard Hot 100 chart. "The Edge of Glory" debuted at number three on the Billboard Hot 100, becoming Gaga's tenth consecutive top-ten single in the United States.

HELP FOR HAITI

On January 15, 2010, Lady Gaga announced on the *Oprah Winfrey Show* that all of the proceeds from the January 24 concert of The Monster Ball Tour in New York would go to Haiti's reconstruction relief fund.

Lady Gaga performed "Judas" on television for the first time on the *Ellen Degeneres Show*.

Born This Way

Born This Way was released on May 23, 2011. The album sold over 1.1 million copies in its first week in the United States. Its launch briefly shut down Amazon.com after Gaga's fans flooded the site to download the new album for a limited-time price of just 99 cents. The album debuted atop the Billboard 200, and topped the charts in more than 23 other countries around the world. While working on the album, Gaga drew inspiration from musicians including Bruce Springsteen, Whitney Houston, and Madonna. The album received rave reviews from music magazines and audiences all over the world. Everyone was still going gaga for Gaga!

Lady Gaga celebrates the launch of her album *Born This Way*.

She Said It

"It's really written by the fans, they really wrote it for me because every night they're funneling so much into me. So I wrote it for them. Born This Way *is all about my little monsters and me, mother monster."*
—In an interview with BBC's *Newsbeat*, 2010

26

Promotional Performances

Gaga worked hard to promote the album leading up to its release. At the 2011 Cannes Film Festival, she sang the song "Judas" for a French television show called *Le Grand Journal*. She performed an **acoustic** version of "Born This Way" on *The Oprah Winfrey Show* in May 2011, along with "You and I." Just four days after the album's release, Gaga performed on *Good Morning America* as part of the Summer Concert Series in Central Park in New York. She shocked the audience by making her entrance to the stage on a zip-line.

Hello, Elton

Gaga paired up with the legendary musician Elton John, who is one of her idols, to record an original duet for the animated feature film *Gnomeo & Juliet.* The song, called "Hello, Hello," was released on February 11, 2011, without Gaga's vocals. The duet version is only featured in the film.

Lady Gaga performs on *Good Morning America* in Central Park in New York City.

27

Queen Monster

Without a doubt, Lady Gaga is one of the most talked about and celebrated women in entertainment and it seems as though she prefers it that way. She is presently putting together a third concert tour and will start rehearsing as soon as possible. The tour is rumored to be named the Born This Way Ball and is planned to kick off in 2012. She is determined to keep influencing the world of music, art, and fashion and will continue to push the limits of her creativity to give her devoted "little monsters" something new to see, hear, and think about. Time and time again, Gaga the Queen Monster has proven that just one voice can make a huge difference in the world.

Timeline

March 28, 1986: Stefani Joanne Angelina Germanotta is born in Yonkers, New York.

1990: Stefani begins taking piano lessons.

2003-2004: Stefani graduates from Convent of the Sacred Heart and was accepted into the Tisch School of the Arts at New York University.

2005: At age 19, Stefani drops out of Tisch.

2005: Stefani forms the band called SGBand.

2006: Stefani launches her first EP called *Red & Blue.*

March 28, 2006: Lady Gaga lands a songwriting deal with Interscope Records on her 20th birthday.

2007: Lady Gaga and Lady Starlight join together and form Lady Gaga and the Starlight Revue. They perform at Lollapalooza in August.

2008: Lady Gaga begins working with the creative team Haus of Gaga.

April, 2008: Gaga's first single "Just Dance" is released and tops the charts landing at No. 1 on Billboard's Hot 100 list.

October 8, 2008: Gaga begins touring with New Kids on the Block reunion tour.

October 28, 2008: *The Fame* is released and Gaga begins The Fame Ball Tour in March of 2009.

2009: Gaga is nominated for a total of nine awards at the MTV Video Music Awards.

October 2009: Gaga receives *Billboard* magazine's Rising Star of 2009 award.

October 26, 2009: The single "Bad Romance" is released and receives rave reviews.

November 18, 2009: *The Fame Monster* is released and The Monster Ball Tour begins.

June 6, 2010: Lady Gaga wears her meat dress to the 2010 MTV Video Music Awards.

May 23, 2011: The album *Born This Way* is released and tops the Billboard Hot 100 chart.

Glossary

acoustic Describing music that has not been electronically modified

activist A person who believes in taking action against something

advocate A person who argues for or supports a cause

AIDS A serious disease of the immune system (Acquired Immune Deficiency Syndrome

debut First appearance

discrimination Treating some people better than others without any fair or proper reason

emulate To try to be like someone

equality The state of being treated equal

exclusive Leaving out others

formidable Very impressive

grossed Amount earned before deductions such as taxes

icon A person or thing in high regard

innovator A person who introduces something new or does something in a new way

inspired Influenced or caused to have particular thoughts or feelings

intolerance The unwillingness to grant people equality, freedom, or other social rights

merchandise Goods that can be bought

persona A role or character

phenomenon A rare or important person or event

prestigious Describing something important or special

renowned Celebrated or famous

revolutionaries People who bring about big or important changes

social justice Equal rights and opportunities in all areas of society

transgendered Someone who identifies with a gender other than the one he or she was born with

Find Out More

Books

Callahan, Maureen. *Poker Face: The Rise and Rise of Lady Gaga*. Hyperion, 2010.

Edwards, Posy. *Lady Gaga: Me & You*. Orion, 2010.

Goodman, Lizzy. *Lady Gaga: Critical Mass Fashion*. St. Martin's Griffin, 2010.

Heos, Bridget. *Lady Gaga* (Megastars). Rosen Central, 2011.

Morgan, Johnny. *Gaga*. Sterling, 2010.

Rafter, Dan and Fowler, Tess. *Fame: Lady Gaga*. Bluewater Productions, 2010.

Websites

Lady Gaga's official site
www.ladygaga.com/

Lady Gaga (ladygaga) on Twitter
http://twitter.com/#!/ladygaga

Lady Gaga on Facebook
www.facebook.com/ladygaga

Lady Gaga: Rolling Stone Music
www.rollingstone.com/music/artists/lady-gaga

Interscope Records: Lady Gaga
www.interscope.com/ladygaga

Index

About the Author

Molly Aloian has written more than 50 nonfiction books for children on a wide variety of topics, including endangered animals, animal life cycles, continents and their geography, mountains and rivers, holidays around the world, and chemistry. When she is not busy writing, she enjoys traveling, hiking, and cooking.